To all my friends
in Kalamazoo.

Dave

HE KIDS
ND SITES OF

Conceived
and supervised by

DAVID FRANK

Photography by
Jennifer Giesey

Designed by
Joe Gugliuzza and David O'Neill

Copyright © 2004 by David Frank
Published in the United States
by ArtStreet LLC
Printed in Italy
ISBN 0-9758971-0-1

Thanks to

Vinny Logan Whitney Jacob B. Keyana Brittany Jake Jacob S. Daniel Anna

Haley Skyler Seth Trevor Kaylee Elijah Mason G. Mason T. Ryan Morgan

Christian Bailey Nick ... and Mrs. Boris.

In 2002, I was asked to illustrate the children's book *I Went to the Party in Kalamazoo* by its author, Ed Shankman. Though I've travelled extensively, I had never been to Kalamazoo.

In 2003, Ed and I received an unexpected letter from students of a first grade class at the Comstock North Elementary School inviting us to their own special party in Kalamazoo! We accepted and flew to Kalamazoo to attend the celebration and spend the weekend. While there, we visited several schools, saw the sights, were interviewed on TV and signed many, many books.

I always felt a thank you was in order for the kindnesses we were shown and also for the success of our first book. *This* book then, *The Kids and Sites of Kalamazoo*, is that thank you. Indeed, it's my very *personal* thank you to all for making the first children's book I ever illustrated a success. I hope you, your families and friends enjoy *The Kids and Sites of Kalamazoo*. Perhaps you know some of the children smiling out at you from these pages. If you're a Kalamazoo resident, I'm sure you'll know many of the locations we photographed.

Thank you Mrs. Boris and your former first grade class. Your invitation was indeed the beginning of this wonderful experience.

And, finally, a very heartfelt thanks to the children of Kalamazoo, whose joy, humor and warmth is so apparent in these pictures.

CELERY FLATS
HISTORIC AREA

Claire

Hannah

Colin

Steven

Colin

Alessondra

Jack

Brent

Owen

Emma, Jordan, Steven & Jillian

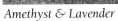

Amethyst & Lavender

Emma

Jillian

Steven

Jordan

DOUGLAS AVE.
FIRE STATION #5

Trent

Wesley, Eric & Garrett

Jessalyn   Madison

Deandre

Thomas

DOUGLAS AVE.
FIRE STATION #5

Kelsey & Elise

Garrett & Jessalyn

I don't know where the rest of my teeth are.
Can't you take my picture anyway?

Amarrea

Trent

Deasia

KARATE KIDS

Cameron   Garrett

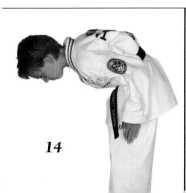

"SHAZAM! No, that's not right. Up, up and away! That's not right, either. Able to leap ... hmm, maybe Batman never said anything cool."

GUESS WHO?

AT THE
PLAYGROUND

Alyssa

Seth

Garrett   *Andrew*

Obejah

*"I look like Shirley Temple?
Who's Shirley Temple?"*

Emma

AT THE
PLAYGROUND

Wyatt

"Look... I can't stand here like this much longer."

Alexander

Madison

Miette

Miniature checker cabs loaned by Hail Kalamazoo.

Obejah

19

Bass & Symphony

GILMORE CAR MUSEUM

GILMORE
CAR MUSEUM

Adrianna

Eliana

Nicholas & Christopher

Zack, Nick & Brad

KALAMAZOO NATURE CENTER

Clare

24

Nyah

Kaitlyn & Elizabeth

William

Ella, Levi & Maddie

Taylor

Marian

CAROUSEL
AT CROSSROADS MALL

Dorrin

Annie

Bailee

Kenny

Benjamin

Monrae

Bryce, Richy & Anna

Remington

Madyson

Jordyn

mmon, Larice, Derrek, Dorrin & Symone

Emily & Benjamin

30

Noah, Nathaniel & Elaine

KALAMAZOO VALLEY

KALAMAZOO VALLEY MUSEUM

Tate & Erin

Caitlin & Cali Rose

Chance   *Caleb*

Charity & Klavion

Justine & Jackie

Alberta & Kierra

Charity

KALAMAZOO VALLEY MUSEUM

Tate, Chance & Caleb

Benjamin

Nathaniel, Noah & Elaine

Daniel

35

Mikayla

Megan & Matthew

Taylor

Mitchell & Jonathon

Derrek & Damon

Marjorie & Laurel

Annemarie

Rachel, Max, Chase & Blake

WESTERN MICHIGAN UNIVERSITY

David

Jared

Taylor

Marjorie

Charlie

Alex

Ashley & Jennifer

Cameron

Megan

Matthew

39

KALAM

Audrey

Ethan

42

Gracie & Jimmy

"Oh my gosh... it's an email from Denzel Washington!"

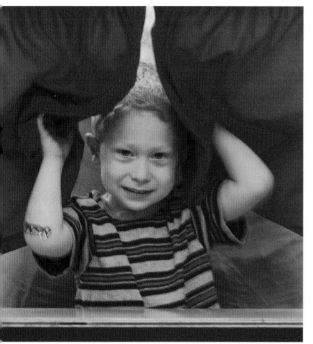

Zachary

Heshima & Imani

Nahshon

Kaitlin & Jared

Michaleh, Riley & Mitchell

Alec & Ethan

*"Hello, Mom?
It's me..."*

*"It's hot. I wore the
wrong clothes..."*

*"No...
don't bring that one.
No, not that one.
No. Uh-uh.
No.
Oh no, not that!"*

Kendal

"No..."

INTERMODAL TRANSPORTATION CENTEI

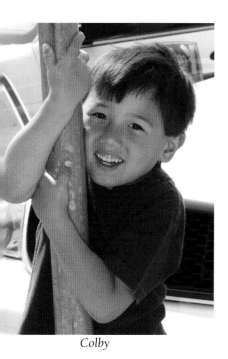

Colby

Tonette

Tiara

Patrick & Derrick

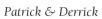

AIR ZOO

Aaron

Julie, Hayley & Megan

Zachary

Patrick & Tom

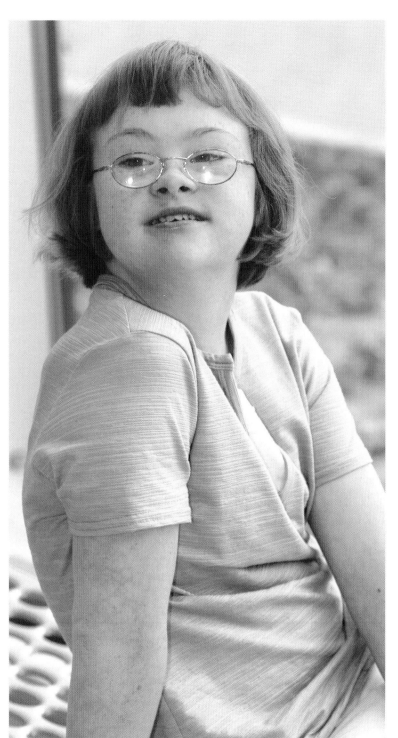

Hillary

Iowa

Ryder, Kari, Kevin, Cassie, Veronica & Erika

Jessica & Dan

Jackie

Noah

Kalyn

Collin

AIR ZOO

Mitchell

Alinah

AIR ZOO

L-R: Ethan, Collin, Emma, Hallie & Cameron

ica

KALAMAZOO MALL

Ella

Hats loaned by The Teacher's Center.

Top: Harrison
Middle: Lindsey, Josh & Alek
Bottom: Gabrielle & Ella

Lindsey   *Gabrielle*

KALAMAZOO KINGS

58

Jace & Greg Wilshire

Sondi & Benjamin

Justin, Cameron, Kyle & Garrett

Justin & David McWatters

ARCADIA
FESTIVAL SITE

Isiah   *Keith*   *Gregory*

Nolan   *Charli*   *Kenny*   *Cameron*   *A.J.*

ARCADIA FESTIVAL SITE

William, Daniel & Clare

Caitlin

Kenny

Isiah, Gregory, Keith, Nolan & A.J.

MLK MEMORIAL PARK

Derrick, Molly & Patrick

Abby K. & Erin

Abby D. & Olivia

"Hmm ... I think this photographer's serious about taking my picture."

Tonette

Shelby

Tiara

*Glasses: $60
T-shirt: $35
Haircut: Priceless.*

EPIC CENTER

Caroline, Hans, Stefanie, Alexander, Haley, Rachel, Blake, Alex

Andrea & A.J.

KAL-HAVEN TRAIL STATE PARK

Piper   Orlando

Ciera Olivia Mrs. Kim Nonthaweth Nikyla   Ivan

BRONSON PARK

Leah

Alex & Carlye

"Uh oh...the Dow just dropped 50 points."

Zoe

"This is either the world's largest baseball, or I'm the world's smallest baseball player."

Garrett

akailah, Danielle, Dayanna, Myron, Jalen, Brandon, Lawrenda, Alexander, Ashtin, Christopher, Isabel, Makayla, Andrew, Brenden, Leanna, Yaniesha

Elizabeth & Andrew

Rachel

Andena & Bryce

Elena & Drew

ROSE PLACE

Rose Place is a unique example of Kalamazoo's historic preservation efforts. In 2003, Rose Place underwent an extensive street enhancement project through a local organization called Partners Building Community. A collaboration of homeowners and private, nonprofit and public partners renovated the streetscape with new curbs, sidewalks, historic street lights, landscaping and recycled brick pavers. A walk down Rose Place is a walk through time, and a proud example of Kalamazoo's strong commitment to urban renewal and historic preservation.

Emma, Amelia & Lucas

Troy & Alicia

EAST GATEWAY

Samantha, Carl & Emily

"Hi, I'm Ryan... the athletic one."

Ryan

"I'm Matthew... the funny one."

"I'm David.
Until this moment,
I thought I was Matthew."

Matthew

David

75

BLUEBERRY
FARM

Founded in 1955 by Roger and Jackie LeDuc, LeDuc Blueberries has been providing quality fruit and a friendly atmosphere for nearly 50 years. The farm is now owned and operated by their sons, Mark and Joe, and their wives, Chris and Chantal. At their farm you'll find clean U-pick fields and a retail store that offers a countless assortment of unusual blueberry items.

Jonathan

Christopher

Logan

Conor & Riley

Olivia & Gabriella

Gracie

Dan

"Boy... this is hard work."

"But these blueberries sure are worth it"

KALAMAZOO COLLEGE

Ava & Lena

Rachael & Lena

Jillian, Elizabeth & Emily

"Eliot introduces the new 'wet look' in photography."

Eliot

Willa

Rachael

CONEY ISLAND

Christian